DARING PLAY

HOW A COURAGEOUS JACKIE ROBINSON TRANSFORMED BASEBALL

by Michael Burgan

Content Adviser: Rick Swaine
Baseball author and member of the
Society for American Baseball Research

COMPASS POINT BOOKS
a capstone imprint

Compass Point Books are published by Capstone,
1710 Roe Crest Drive, North Mankato, Minnesota 56003
www.mycapstone.com

Editor: Catherine Neitge
Designers: Tracy Davies McCabe and Catherine Neitge
Media Researcher: Eric Gohl
Library Consultant: Kathleen Baxter
Production Specialist: Lori Barbeau

Image Credits
AP Photo: 25, 32, 45, John Rooney, 51, Marty Lederhandler, 29; Corbis: Bettmann,
cover, 11, 13, 19, 37, 38, 39, 41, 53, 59 (bottom); David R. Wagner: 21; Getty
Images: Gado/*Afro* Newspaper, 20, 46, Hulton Archive, 15, 26, 27, 55, 56 (top),
J. R. Eyerman, 16, Lambert, 35, The LIFE Picture Collection/Grey Villet, 36, The LIFE
Picture Collection/Herb Scharfman, 50, MLB Photos, 7, *New York Daily News* Archive,
34, *New York Daily News* Archive/Frank Hurley, 31, Robert Riger, 44, Rogers Photo
Archive, 10, Transcendental Graphics, 5, 24, 28; Library of Congress: 57 (bottom);
Newscom: Everett Collection, 57 (top), Icon SMI, 58, Icon SMI/Panworld Sports, 8,
Icon SMI/TSN, 6, 56 (bottom), KRT/Michael Hogue, 23, Reuters/Jonathan Ernst, 54,
Splash News/London Ent, 49; Shutterstock: catwalker, 48, Krylova Ksenia, 59 (top),
Leonard Zhukovsky, 43

Library of Congress Cataloging-in-Publication Data
Cataloging-in-publication information is on file with the Library of Congress.
ISBN 978-0-7565-5291-6 (library binding)
ISBN 978-0-7565-5295-4 (paperback)
ISBN 978-0-7565-5299-2 (ebook PDF)

Printed in the United States of America, in Stevens Point Wisconsin.
092015   009222WZS16

TABLEOFCONTENTS

Chapter One

PLAYING FOR THE CHAMPIONSHIP

With almost 64,000 fans filling Yankee Stadium, Jackie Robinson was ready to play. His Brooklyn Dodgers had reached the World Series four times during Robinson's career. Each time they had faced the powerful New York Yankees. Each time Robinson and his teammates had ended their season watching the Yankees celebrate another World Series title, making them the champions of Major League Baseball. Would the 1955 World Series be different?

To the Dodgers and their fans, the Yankees were not just another team. Although the two teams played in different leagues and different parts of New York City, they were still rivals. The World Series gave fans of both the Yankees and the Dodgers a chance to see their favorite teams face off, with the winners getting to brag they were the best team in the city, not to mention the major leagues.

But for the Brooklyn team, the bragging had been missing. They had never won a World Series and had only played in three before Robinson joined the team. The Yankees, meanwhile, had won 16 World Series before 1955, including five in a row from 1949 to 1953. Dodger fans affectionately called their team "Dem Bums," but it was frustrating to watch the Dodgers lose season after season. All the fans could say was "Wait 'til next year."

A decade before the 1955 World Series, Robinson's

The stars of the 1955 Brooklyn Dodgers were ready to take the field: Carl Furillo (from left), Jackie Robinson, Roy Campanella, Pee Wee Reese, Duke Snider, Preacher Roe, and Gil Hodges.

baseball skills and personality attracted the attention of Branch Rickey, the president, general manager, and part owner of the Dodgers. Rickey had decided that it was time for the major leagues to recruit their first African-American player. Rickey knew that the man chosen to break the "color line" that kept talented blacks out of the league had to be special. Racism was common across the country, and in many southern states

segregation was a fact of life. African-Americans weren't allowed as guests in hotels and restaurants meant for white customers. Most blacks in the South could not vote, and their children went to inferior schools.

Rickey wanted the first black player to be smart, brave, and able to withstand racism without reacting angrily. The player might seethe inside, but he would not respond to the taunts and discrimination he would face. Rickey was sure Robinson was the player he wanted. Yet after Robinson became a Dodger—and usually managed to

Before Jackie Robinson (left) moved up to the major league Dodgers, Branch Rickey signed him to a contract on October 23, 1945, to play with the Montreal Royals, the Dodgers' top minor league team.

Robinson officially broke the color line April 15, 1947, when he made his major league debut against the Boston Braves at Ebbets Field in Brooklyn.

keep his feelings inside—his self-respect and desire to win sometimes came to the surface. When he spoke his mind about racial issues or the treatment he received, some whites thought he was complaining too much. Stepping to the plate or taking his position on the field, Robinson often heard boos. A sportswriter told him that the press and some fans disliked him because he was too aggressive. Few white players would have been criticized for that, or for speaking honestly about their treatment, as Robinson often did.

In 1947 Robinson became the first major league player to receive the Rookie of the Year award.

Robinson played a huge role in getting the Dodgers into the World Series starting in 1947, his first year in the big leagues. He was a good hitter and an excellent fielder.

"Jackie Robinson was born to play and excel in the awful pressure of a World Series."

He played wherever the Dodgers needed him, moving from second base to third or first. Although a natural infielder, he played more than 150 games in the outfield to help his team. Robinson was also fast and ready to take risks on the base paths when necessary. Just as important as his athletic skill was his playing style. He always played hard and did anything he could to win. "Above anything else," he once said, "I hate to lose."

Before the 1955 season began, however, he didn't know how long he could keep playing. Although still a fast runner, he had slowed down a bit. And injuries sometimes limited his playing time. He began thinking about life beyond baseball.

Robinson missed nearly one-third of the 1955 season because of injuries and age. But as the postseason approached, he was in better health and playing well. "I made up my mind to go out there and hustle," he said. He felt that his energy had helped inspire his teammates to win the National League pennant.

Despite his contributions, some baseball experts wondered whether Robinson would be a starting player in Game 1 of the World Series against the Yankees. Former Dodgers manager Leo Durocher had managed Robinson in Brooklyn and had seen him play while running the New York Giants, the city's other team. The thought of not starting Robinson was crazy, Durocher said. "Jackie Robinson was born to play and excel in the awful pressure of a World Series." When Brooklyn's starting lineup for

Game 1 was announced September 28, Robinson was in it, playing third base.

The Dodgers scored first, getting two runs in the top of the second inning. Robinson contributed with a triple and then scored on a single by Don Zimmer. The Yankees tied

THE SLOW PACE OF INTEGRATION

Roy Campanella (from left) and Don Newcombe joined Robinson as stars of the Brooklyn Dodgers.

Major League Baseball and sports historians note that while Jackie Robinson made history, he was not the first black to play professional baseball on a team with whites. Robinson made history by breaking the color line that had been in force since the late 1800s. The color line meant that only whites were allowed to play for the major league teams and for the minor league teams that helped train their players.

During the 1870s Bud Fowler became the first African-American known to play professionally for a white club. Like Robinson, Fowler was a skilled infielder. The first black player known to play regularly in a major league was Moses Fleetwood Walker, a catcher. He played for Toledo, which joined one of the first major leagues, the American Association, in 1884. Soon after, however, the color line returned to baseball. Historians place much of the blame on Adrian "Cap" Anson, the manager and star player of the National League team in Chicago now called the Cubs. Anson had strong racist views and refused to allow his team to play against Walker's team or any other team with an African-American player. By the end of the century, no blacks played in the major leagues or for the top minor league teams.

Robinson's success with the Brooklyn Dodgers answered any questions about whether African-Americans deserved to be in the major leagues. Honest baseball players and fans had known the answer for some time. White stars often played against stars of the Negro Leagues, teams made up of African-American players. White players and fans saw that the talents of the top black players matched or exceeded those of many white major leaguers. Even so, most major league clubs were slow to sign black players. By 1952 only five other teams had joined the Dodgers in integrating their rosters—the Cleveland Indians, St. Louis Browns, New York Giants, Boston Braves, and Chicago White Sox.

Even when teams did sign black players, they might have just one, though by 1949 the Dodgers had three black stars. Joining Robinson were pitcher Don Newcombe and catcher Roy Campanella. The last team to integrate was the Boston Red Sox, which did not have a black player on its roster until 1959. The percentage of African-American players held steady from the early 1970s to the mid-1990s at from 16 to 19 percent. Since then it has fallen to about 7 percent. At the same time, the percentage of Latino players has risen to about 27 percent.

the score in the bottom of the inning. In the third, Brooklyn scored again, only to see the Yankees once again tie it. Over the next three innings, the Yankees took a three-run lead. The score was still 6-3 in the eighth when Robinson came to the plate with one out and a man on first. He once again faced the Yankees' Whitey Ford, one of the top pitchers in the game. Robinson hit a ground ball that third baseman Gil McDougald could not field cleanly. Robinson reached second on the error, then went to third on a sacrifice fly. The sacrifice had scored the runner ahead of him, so now, with the score 6-4 and two outs, Robinson looked at home plate just 90 feet (27 meters) away.

Robinson later wrote that he stood on third base thinking this could be his last year in baseball, his last chance to help Brooklyn win a World Series and defeat their New York rivals. "I suddenly decided to shake things up," Robinson wrote. "It was not the best baseball strategy to steal home with our team two runs behind, but I just took off and did it."

What happened when Jackie Robinson stole home in the World Series led to a controversial call at the plate. It also led to one of the most famous photographs from Robinson's historic career.

Robinson slides under the mitt of Yankee catcher Yogi Berra to steal home in the 1955 World Series in one of baseball's most famous photographs.

ChapterTwo
BREAKING THE COLOR BARRIER

Jackie Robinson's path to the major leagues and the 1955 World Series began in a small house near Cairo, Georgia. Jack Roosevelt Robinson was born January 31, 1919. His middle name was in honor of President Theodore Roosevelt, who had died just a few weeks before. Roosevelt had spoken out against racism, but his policies did not end the segregation common in Georgia and other former slave states.

Jack, as his family called him, was the grandson of slaves, and his father, Jerry, worked as a sharecropper. A white farmer let Jerry Robinson use some of his land and gave him supplies, along with a place for the Robinsons to live. In return, Robinson gave half of what he grew to the landowner.

Jack was the youngest of five children. His father left the family shortly after Jack was born. Jack's mother, Mallie Robinson, struggled to raise her family, and at the urging of her half-brother moved the family to California. Jackie was not quite 18 months old when the Robinsons arrived in Pasadena, a suburb of Los Angeles.

Through hard work, Mallie Robinson was able to save money and buy her family a home. But she still struggled at times to feed her family. Jackie Robinson later wrote that when his mother wasn't working, she taught her children "the importance of family unity, religion, and kindness toward others."

Mallie Robinson posed for a family portrait in 1925 with her children (from left) Mack, Jackie, Edgar, Willa Mae, and Frank.

The first African-Americans had come to Pasadena in the 1880s. Many worked as household help for whites. Later, during World War I, more found jobs at mills and factories. The African-Americans created their own community, and they never received equal treatment from the much larger white population. When a public pool opened, blacks were allowed to swim in it only one day a week.

Blacks were kept from living in certain neighborhoods, and many of the Robinsons' white neighbors didn't welcome them. As a boy, young Jack heard the insults that many whites hurled at African-Americans.

Measured by the amount of racial violence, though, Pasadena was an improvement over rural Georgia. And the schools were integrated, so Jack received roughly the same education white children did. He sometimes hung out with boys who got into trouble, either by stealing small items or throwing dirt clods at passing cars. Robinson later credited his Christian faith with helping him avoid a life of crime. But something else also helped. From a young age, he showed remarkable athletic talent. He focused much of his life on several sports, including baseball.

By the time he was in high school, Robinson was already an excellent infielder. He was also a star in track, basketball, and football. Outside of school, he played tennis. In every sport, he relied on his speed and determination to win. Other players saw his talents, he later wrote, and "They decided that I was the best man to beat. I enjoyed having that kind of reputation, but I was also very much aware of the importance of being a team man, not jeopardizing my team's chances simply to get the spotlight."

Robinson entered Pasadena Junior College in 1937 and continued to excel in all his sports. His daring baserunning soon drew attention. In one game, after reaching first base, he proceeded to steal second, third, and home to score a run. Later that year, playing in a city league, he often repeated that feat.

He was also the quarterback for Pasadena Junior College's football team. At times he heard racist taunts, and even some of his white teammates showed prejudice. Robinson's reactions varied. He once challenged a white student to a fight for making racist comments, and the man backed down. To deal with his teammates, Robinson went to his coach and threatened to leave Pasadena if the coach did not take action. The coach did, restoring harmony among the team's white and black players.

Robinson's success in sports drew the attention of major four-year colleges. In 1939 he enrolled at the University of California at Los Angeles (UCLA). He wanted to concentrate on football and track but ended up playing baseball and basketball too. Local newspapers began calling him Jackie, and the name stuck. Some of his greatest heroics came in football. Robinson showed his versatility in returning kicks, running the ball, and throwing and catching passes.

He spent two years at UCLA, leaving before receiving a degree. He wanted to go to work to make money to help his family. For a while he worked with kids, teaching them sports. Then he moved to Hawaii to play minor league football. After the 1941 season ended in November, Robinson went back to California. During his trip home, Japan attacked the U.S. Navy base in Pearl Harbor, Hawaii. Soon the United States was at war, and Robinson was in the U.S. Army.

Robinson was sent to Fort Riley, Kansas, for training and was assigned to a cavalry unit. He excelled in the military the same way he had in athletics. He was an expert rifleman, and he had the intelligence and drive that the Army liked in its officers. But when he applied for Officer Candidate School (OCS), he was turned down. Robinson faced racism on the baseball field too. He tried to join Fort Riley's baseball team, but he was told that blacks were not allowed to play.

While at the Army camp, Robinson met one of the

Robinson was a star football player at UCLA. He was the school's first athlete to earn letters in four sports.

greatest athletes of the day, the boxer Joe Louis. He had won the heavyweight championship in 1937 and hadn't lost since. Both black and white boxing fans admired his skills in the ring. Like professional athletes in many sports, Louis had volunteered for the military. He was willing to do his part for his country, even though that country sometimes discriminated against him and other African-Americans.

Louis supported Robinson's quest to attend Officer Candidate School, and in November 1942 the Army

finally agreed to let Robinson and other blacks go to OCS.
Robinson completed the training and in January 1943
earned the rank of second lieutenant. Being an officer,
though, wasn't enough for Fort Riley's baseball team to
let him play. Robinson accepted the insult without saying
a word.

The Army was reluctant to send black units into
combat overseas, so Robinson stayed at Fort Riley. Also
holding him back was an old injury to his ankle, which he
had hurt again in the Army. But in April 1944 Robinson
was ordered to Camp Hood, Texas.

SEGREGATION IN THE MILITARY

Black soldiers served gallantly during the Revolution but did not receive equal treatment for hundreds of years.

During the American Revolution, some blacks, both slaves and free, fought alongside whites against the British to win America's independence. But by the start of World War II, the U.S. military was segregated. Blacks and whites had separate units, though the black units were usually led by white officers. When the war in Europe began in 1939, the Army had only five black officers, three of whom were chaplains. Most black troops belonged to service units, whose duties included transporting supplies and cooking meals.

Racists in the military did not think blacks had the intelligence or skills to take part in combat. That attitude even extended to U.S. Secretary of War Henry Stimson. He wrote, "There is a consensus that colored units are inferior to the performance of white troops, except for service duties." President Harry Truman ordered the military to integrate in 1948, but some segregation still remained when the United States entered the Korean War in 1950.

At Camp Hood, Robinson got tangled up in a racial incident that almost ended his military career. Laws at the time forced blacks in some states to ride at the back of buses, away from whites. On one bus trip, Robinson sat in the middle, next to a woman he knew. Robinson refused to obey the driver's order that he move to the back of the bus. The driver called in the military police, and Robinson was soon being questioned by a white officer. The questioning did not go well, as Robinson tried to explain the situation.

The officer did not like Robinson's attitude, and several weeks later, Robinson found himself under arrest for disrespecting and disobeying an officer. He believed he had been charged because he was black.

Robinson faced a court-martial. Losing the military trial could mean jail time and a dishonorable discharge from the Army. Robinson's lawyer, though, was able to show that he had behaved properly and had not violated Army regulations. Robinson was found not guilty, but he soon asked to be let out of the Army because of his ankle injury. The Army agreed, and he was honorably discharged.

Despite the injury, Robinson was still healthy enough to play baseball, and in 1945 he joined the Kansas City Monarchs of the Negro Leagues. He was grateful for the money he earned, but life on the road was hard. He disliked traveling long distances by bus, staying in cheap hotels, and scrambling to find food when restaurants refused to serve blacks. He also missed his girlfriend, Rachel, whom he'd met while at UCLA and who was still in California. While

Robinson played for the Kansas City Monarchs, one of the top teams in the Negro Leagues.

enduring the hardships, Robinson also knew that life was much better for the white players in the major leagues.

As he played for the Monarchs, Robinson didn't know that in Brooklyn, the Dodgers' Branch Rickey had a plan. Rickey thought the time had come to integrate baseball. One of the black players he was interested in was Robinson.

Rickey arranged for Robinson to come to Brooklyn to meet with him. Robinson thought the Dodgers president

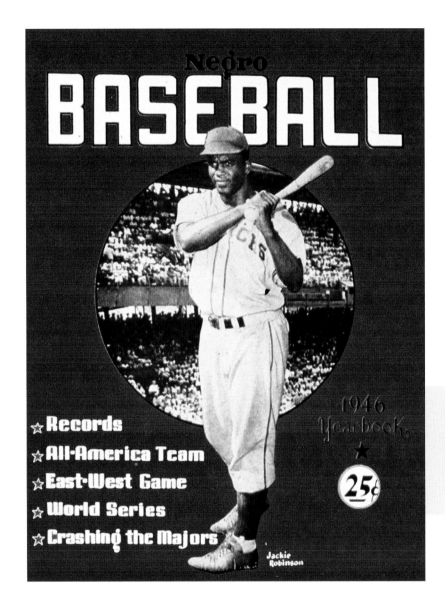

wanted him to play for an all-black team sponsored by the Dodgers. Instead, Rickey told him he wanted him to be the first black player in the major leagues. First he would play for the Dodgers' top farm team, the Montreal Royals of the International League. Then, if Robinson proved his talents, he would move up to the Dodgers. Robinson's reaction? "I was thrilled, scared and excited. ... Most of all, I was speechless." But he managed to say yes.

After hitting a three-run homer in his first game for Montreal, Robinson was congratulated by teammate George Shuba. The photo, said *The New York Times*, "has endured as a portrait of racial tolerance."

The next year Robinson was in Montreal, the largest city in the Canadian province of Quebec. He was the first African-American known to play for a top-level minor league team since the 1800s. Playing against teams based in the United States, Robinson sometimes heard racial slurs. But his teammates accepted him, and so did the fans in Montreal. In his first year of professional baseball, Robinson led the International League with a

.349 batting average and 113 runs scored. He also stole 40 bases and helped the Royals win the league championship. After that impressive start, Rickey decided that Robinson would join the Dodgers.

Even before Robinson played his first major league game, he faced challenges. Several of his teammates were racists. They told Rickey they would not play with a black teammate. Rickey and manager Leo Durocher, however, supported Robinson. So on Opening Day, April 15, 1947, Robinson emerged from the Dodgers dugout at Ebbets Field, the team's home stadium, to play first base.

Robinson helped Montreal win the International League by an impressive 19½ games.

On Opening Day 1947 Robinson (right) posed with teammates on the steps of the Dodgers dugout. They are (from left) Johnny Jorgensen, Pee Wee Reese, and Eddie Stanky.

A few days earlier a headline in the *Boston Chronicle*, a black-owned newspaper, declared, "Triumph of Whole Race Seen in Jackie's Debut in Major League Ball."

Robinson knew that other blacks wanted him to succeed—and that many whites hoped he failed. The feelings of some whites went even deeper—some made death threats against him. He also faced the expected racial slurs, and opposing players sometimes slid into him hard. One player used his spiked shoes to draw blood from Robinson's leg. He did not react, and as the season went on, more of his teammates supported him against

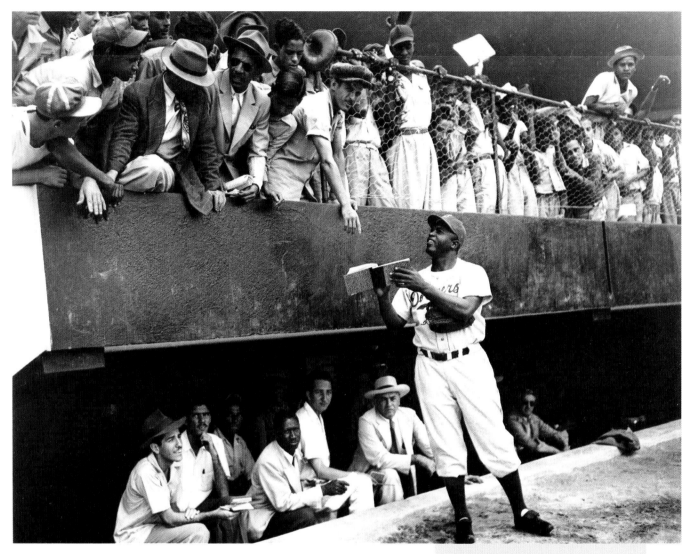

the racists he encountered. "I had started the season as a lonely man," he said. "I ended it feeling like a member of a solid team."

The Dodgers won the National League pennant, and Robinson was named baseball's Rookie of the Year. The Dodgers lost the World Series to the Yankees, but Robinson had earned the respect of Americans, both black and white. *Time* magazine put him on the cover of its September 22, 1947, issue. After the season a survey found him to be the second most famous man in the country,

Robinson led the league with 37 steals when he was named Most Valuable Player in 1949.

ahead of President Harry Truman and several heroes of World War II. (The top spot went to singer Bing Crosby.)

In the seasons that followed, Robinson got even better. In 1949 he led the National League with a batting average of .342, appeared in the first of his six All-Star games, and was named the league's Most Valuable Player. And as he had done since college, he rattled opposing pitchers with his daring baserunning—just as he hoped to do to Whitey Ford in Game 1 of the 1955 World Series.

ChapterThree
STEALING HOME

Jackie Robinson stood on third with two outs in the top of the eighth inning in Game 1 of the 1955 World Series. Pinch hitter Frank Kellert stepped to the plate. On the first pitch, Robinson danced down the base line a bit, then headed back as Kellert took a ball. Whitey Ford, at least one baseball writer thought, had slowed his delivery a bit, perhaps trying to focus on keeping Robinson from scoring. If Robinson noticed the slower delivery, it might have influenced his decision to run. Years later he wrote, "I was just tired of waiting." He was tired of waiting to win a World Series.

Usually when runners try to steal a base, they have received a signal from their manager, relayed through one of the coaches on the field. But this time Robinson took off on his own. He had two advantages. One was the element of surprise—runners almost never tried to steal home with two outs when their club was behind. Making the third out on the steal attempt would take away the chance of scoring on a hit. The other advantage: Ford was left-handed, so his back was to third base. He might not see Robinson begin his daring dash to the plate.

But Yankee catcher Yogi Berra did, and he stepped toward the plate to take Ford's pitch. Kellert waited until Robinson was close to the plate and then stepped back slightly from the batter's box. Robinson slid in, Berra tagged him, and umpire Bill Summers ruled Robinson safe. Robinson calmly got up and jogged to the Dodgers dugout with the score 6-5 in the

Umpire Bill Summers called Robinson safe after the daring player stole home. An outraged Yogi Berra argued the call, creating what *The New York Times* called "one of the enduring images of an on-the-field tantrum."

Yankees' favor. Berra, meanwhile, jumped up, ripped off his face mask, and bounced up and down near Summers, arguing the call. Summers stepped away from the angry catcher, and Berra followed him. As *The New York Times* reported, Berra "almost blew a gasket" over the call. He and

other Yankees might have been upset too, because their second baseman, Billy Martin, had been called out when he had tried to steal home a few innings earlier. In the end,

The baseball passes in front of him as Robinson races toward home plate in his successful steal in the eighth inning of Game 1.

though, Robinson's run didn't change the outcome of the game. The Yankees held on to win 6-5.

For Robinson, that steal marked the 18th time in his career that he had stolen home. (He would steal home two more times the next season.) It was just the ninth time a player had done it in a World Series. Robinson's skill at making that rare play even found its way into a song about him. The 1949 song "Did You See Jackie Robinson Hit That Ball?" includes the words "and that ain't all. He stole home." But his steal in the 1955 World Series would be the one people remembered.

Part of the reason was the controversy over umpire Bill Summers' safe call. Some of it was Robinson's decision to run at all. After the game reporters confronted Robinson in the locker room. Some seemed to question the wisdom of his running with two outs. "When they give me the run I'm certainly going to take it," Robinson said. "The only ridiculous thing about that play was the Yankees' squawking about me being called safe."

Something else made this steal memorable. As Robinson slid across home plate, photographers captured the moment. Herb Scharfman snapped the shutter release on his Speed Graphic camera, and a historic photo was born. While photographers had taken pictures of some of Robinson's other steals of home, this one became the most famous. The image clearly shows Berra making the tag, but there's no way to tell whether it came before or after Robinson touched the plate.

Part of the picture's fame, of course, comes from when it was taken—during a World Series between rival clubs.

And the disputed nature of the play added to its importance. But the shot also seemed to sum up the way Robinson had lived his life before and after breaking baseball's color barrier. He acted on his own, doing what he thought was right. He took risks. He used his talents the best way he knew how.

The controversy over Robinson's stealing home in the World Series never went away. Until he died in 2015, Yogi Berra insisted that he had tagged Robinson before he slid across the plate. He even autographed a photo of the famous steal for President Barack Obama. "Dear Mr. President," Berra wrote. "He was out!" Helping to fuel the debate was a

THE CAMERA OF CHOICE

From the 1930s through the 1950s, newspaper photographers across the United States relied on the Speed Graphic camera to do their job. Sports photographers liked the camera because it was easy to carry and well made.

They were so tough that U.S. military photographers used Speed Graphics during World War II. (Photographer Joe Rosenthal took the famous 1945 image of Marines raising the U.S. flag over Iwo Jima with a Speed Graphic.)

One of the camera's distinguishing features was its round silver bulb holder. When the bulb flashed, it cast a bluish-white light. The camera used film that created negatives that were 4 inches by 5 inches (10 centimeters by 13 centimeters), resulting in great detail in the final picture.

But since they were using film, photographers couldn't take multiple shots per second as today's sports photographers do. So good timing—or good luck—was crucial for getting a historic shot.

Newspaper photographers the world over used the heavy Speed Graphic cameras to produce beautiful detailed shots.

film clip of the play, which is available on YouTube. Berra, among others, watched the replay many times, and he had this to say in 2003: "Jackie was out in 1955, he was out when I saw the replay 20 years ago, and he's still out!"

A picture taken a few days after the game shows both players smiling as Berra supposedly explains to Robinson

how he made the tag. But just as Berra long insisted that Robinson was out, umpire Bill Summers equally insisted that he had made the right call. Like Berra, he watched replays of the play years later. "See that?" he told his daughter. "I was right."

Herb Scharfman was no stranger to Robinson and the Dodgers. He had photographed his first Brooklyn game more than 16 years earlier, almost by accident. In 1932 Scharfman joined International News Service (INS), which provided

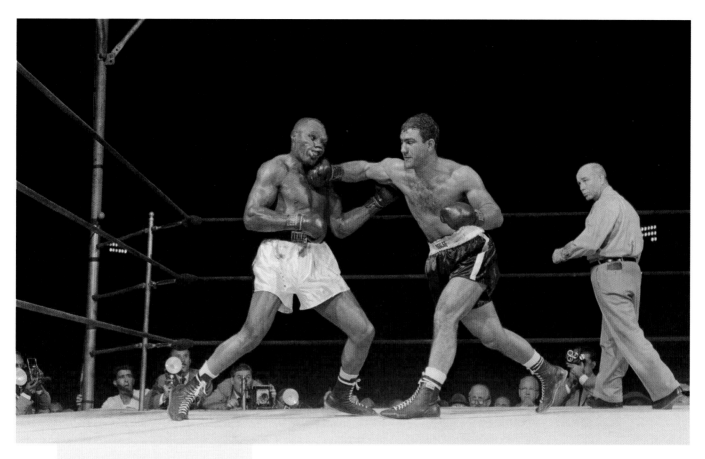

Herb Scharfman's camera caught Jersey Joe Wolcott's distorted face under the force of a blow from boxer Rocky Marciano in 1952.

stories and photographs to newspapers across the United States. He worked in the photo division as a motorcycle messenger. With money he earned and a loan, he bought a Speed Graphic camera and took pictures as a hobby. In 1939 an INS photo editor asked whether he owned a suit. Scharfman said yes, and the editor sent him to Ebbets Field to shoot that day's baseball game between the Brooklyn Dodgers and the Philadelphia Phillies. After that, Scharfman became a full-time sports photographer for INS. In that job he took another historic sports shot, one of boxer Rocky Marciano delivering a punch that ended the boxing career of Jersey Joe Wolcott. Scharfman snapped the picture at the exact moment the punch wildly distorted Wolcott's face.

Scharfman also traveled with the Dodgers to their spring training camp in Florida. Taking pictures away from the pressures of the long, grueling season, he became friendly with several of the players, including Robinson. A shot Scharfman took in 1951 in Florida shows Robinson playing with his son Jackie Jr. The start of the caption that ran with the picture reads, "Giving Dad a Few Pointers."

Scharfman took a shot with a more serious message in 1953. It showed Robinson shaking hands with teammate Billy Cox at a time when racial tension seemed to be brewing among the Dodgers. Charlie Dressen, manager at the time, announced at the start of spring training that Billy Cox would no longer start at third base and instead would be a

A photo of smiling teammates Jackie Robinson and Billy Cox helped preserve harmony in the Dodgers clubhouse.

utility player, filling in at various positions for other players. Cox was considered an outstanding third baseman and was not happy with the move. Perhaps also upsetting Cox was that Robinson would move to third base to make room for second baseman Junior Gilliam, who was black. Robinson and other Dodgers told reporters they didn't think race was an issue. But to Walter O'Malley, the team's new president, Scharfman's picture of Cox and Robinson was strong visual proof of harmony on the team. O'Malley was a part owner of the Dodgers and had replaced Branch Rickey. He wrote to Scharfman in a letter, "Your picture … was the best answer to all the tripe written about discrimination on this club. That is just what they say, a good picture never lies."

Scharfman was on the job for the remaining games of the 1955 World Series, as the Dodgers tried to overcome the opening game loss. Robinson thought that even though the Yankees took the first game, his steal of home might have been a spark for the other Dodgers. Whatever caused it, he wrote, "the team had new fire." But not enough to win Game 2, and the Yankees took it 4-2.

The Series then moved from Yankee Stadium to Ebbets Field. In Game 3 Robinson had two hits, including a double that ended up with him on third after Yankee outfielder Elston Howard threw to the wrong base. Earlier in the game, as a runner at third, Robinson had darted back and forth off the bag, trying to distract Yankee pitcher Bob Turley and catcher Berra. With the memory of Game 1 still fresh, the Yankees couldn't know whether Robinson was just teasing or preparing for another theft of home. After the game, a newspaper headline read, "Aging Robinson Sets Dodgers Afire."

The Dodgers won that game 8-3 and then took the next two on their home field. With the Series back in the Bronx, the Dodgers lost Game 6, forcing a deciding Game 7. Robinson sat out that pivotal game, though today no one is sure why. He was still feeling pain from past injuries, but he had played every inning of the first six games. Maybe Dodgers manager Walter Alston thought he had not performed well enough at the plate. Robinson had only managed four hits in the first six games. Also, the manager and his star player did not have the friendliest relationship. At the end of the 1954 season, Robinson later wrote, he and Alston "began to get into minor hassles and exchange impulsive ill-tempered words." Early in the 1955 season, an argument between Alston and Robinson

The 1955 Dodgers, including Jackie Robinson (center, arms outstretched), rushed to the mound after claiming their first World Series championship, beating the Yankees four games to three.

turned into "a shouting match that seemed destined to end in a physical fight."

Decades later, reporters asked Rachel Robinson why her husband had sat out that important Game 7. "I don't know why Jack didn't play," she said. "I really don't know." So from the bench Robinson watched the Dodgers win 2-0 and finally beat the Yankees for the championship. He said later, "It was one of the greatest thrills of my life to be finally on a World Series winner."

That championship would be the only one the Brooklyn Dodgers ever won. Future World Series wins would come after the Dodgers had moved across the country to Los Angeles. The 1955 Series would be remembered for the Brooklyn win, for the close play between the New York rivals, and for perhaps the most famous steal of home ever seen in baseball.

Chapter Four

ENDURING LEGACIES

Although he didn't play in that final World Series game, Jackie Robinson still joyously celebrated with his teammates. One of the few players still left on the Dodgers from Robinson's historic first year was shortstop Pee Wee Reese. In 1947 Reese had been one of the few southerners on the team who refused to sign a petition against Robinson's playing for the Dodgers. Reese didn't think of it as a grand statement for civil rights—he just thought Robinson had a right to earn a living in baseball too.

But at some point either that season or the next—historical accounts differ—Reese made a point of going over to Robinson in front of a hostile crowd and putting his arm around him as a sign of friendship. Reese later said, "I was just trying to make the world a little bit better. That's what you're supposed to do with your life, isn't it?" Robinson, recalling the incident, said, "I never felt alone on a baseball field again." After that the two men turned many double plays together when Robinson was at his preferred spot of second base.

The 1956 season was the last that Robinson and Reese played together. Robinson was 37, and he still faced racism. After he argued with an umpire, the National League fined Robinson. Some people believed that a white player would not have been fined for the same thing. Outside baseball, racism was still strong, as some whites reacted against

"I was just trying to make the world a little bit better. That's what you're supposed to do with your life, isn't it?"

The Jackie Robinson and Pee Wee Reese monument was unveiled in Brooklyn in 2005. The bronze statue captures the moment when Reese threw his arm around his new teammate in a show of support for Major League Baseball's first black player.

the rising call for equality for blacks. Robinson followed the events of the growing civil rights movement and sometimes spoke out against continuing segregation.

His age and nagging injuries didn't keep Robinson from achieving better statistics at the plate compared with his performance in 1955. And he was able to help the Dodgers win the pennant again, though they lost to the Yankees in the 1956 World Series. Even so, he had been thinking about retiring since 1954. After the 1956 season, when he received a good job offer outside baseball, Robinson knew the time had come to leave the game. "The way I figured it," he later wrote, "I was even with baseball and baseball with me. The game had done much for me, and I had done much for it." Baseball honored his

Hands curled as if around a baseball bat, Robinson stood with his family shortly after being elected to the National Baseball Hall of Fame in 1962. From left are wife, Rachel, Jackie Jr., 15, David, 9, and Sharon, 12.

contributions in 1962, when Robinson became the first African-American inducted into the National Baseball Hall of Fame. He was elected on the first ballot.

Robinson began his business career with Chock Full o' Nuts. The New York-based company owned coffee shops and sold its coffee in stores. During seven years with the company, Robinson also became more involved with the National Association for the Advancement of Colored People (NAACP) and its fight for equality for

HONORED FOR HIS ACTIONS AND CHARACTER

Robinson held an NAACP placard and marched in support of southern black students in 1955.

One of the leading organizations fighting for civil rights for blacks was, and still is, the NAACP. Right after the 1947 season, an NAACP chapter in California honored Robinson for breaking the color barrier, saying he had "knock[ed] prejudice clear out of a Big League Ball Park!" At that time Robinson was not actively involved in the civil rights movement, though he later worked with the National Conference of Christians and Jews. The group stressed social justice and the idea that people of all religious and racial backgrounds should be kind to each other and work together.

By 1955, though, Robinson was more focused on civil rights. In 1956 he received the NAACP's highest honor, the Spingarn Medal. It is awarded each year for outstanding achievement by an African-American. Robinson was the first athlete to receive the award. The NAACP said, "the entire nation is indebted to him for his pioneer role in breaking the color bar in organized baseball." Robinson served on the NAACP's board of directors for many years and helped raise money for the group.

African-Americans. Blacks in the South sometimes faced violence as they marched for civil rights or tried to exercise their right to vote. In a public statement in 1964, Robinson wrote, "I am solidly committed to the peaceful, non-violent mass action of the Negro people in pursuit of long-overdue justice." Unfortunately, it was white police officers who sometimes used violence against peaceful blacks.

Robinson continued to work for justice and equality for African-Americans. He owned a construction company that built low- and moderate-income housing. But Robinson battled health problems, including diabetes and heart disease. He died of a heart attack on October 24, 1972, at age 53. Nine days earlier, at a World Series game he attended, Major League Baseball had marked the 25th anniversary of his breaking the color line.

Robinson's obituary in *The New York Times* said that in terms of his impact on U.S. society, Robinson was "perhaps America's most significant athlete." The *Times* article noted Robinson's many steals of home, but only gave details about one of them—the steal in Game 1 of the 1955 World Series. The paper also quoted Robinson describing the impact of his running ability—or simply the threat that he would run: "I think my value to the Dodgers was disruption—making the pitcher concentrate on me instead of on my teammate who was at bat at the time."

In the decades that followed, Major League Baseball and the nation honored Robinson. In 1982 he was the first baseball player to appear on a U.S. postage stamp.

Robinson was "perhaps America's most significant athlete."

He appeared on another stamp in 1999, sliding into home. The stamp's image is similar to a photo of Robinson stealing home, though not Herb Scharfman's famous picture. He appeared on yet another stamp in 2000.

President Ronald Reagan in 1984 awarded Robinson the Medal of Freedom, the highest honor a U.S. civilian can receive. In 1997 the government issued gold and silver coins to mark the 50th anniversary of Robinson's appearance in the major leagues. The same year, Major League Baseball announced that Robinson's number, 42, would be retired by all teams. No player would be issued that number again. Starting in 2004, every major league player, coach, and manager on the field has worn a uniform with the number 42 on April 15, Jackie Robinson Day, which is celebrated at baseball stadiums throughout the country.

After 1956, as Jackie Robinson pursued business interests and fought for civil rights, Herb Scharfman continued taking sports pictures. In 1958 the Dodgers moved from Brooklyn to Los Angeles, becoming one of the first major league teams on the West Coast. (The Giants moved from New York to San Francisco the same year.) The move also ended the Yankee-Dodgers rivalry of Robinson's day. Scharfman, though, still went to Florida every March for Dodgers spring training.

The year the Dodgers moved, International News Service merged with another news organization to form United Press International. Scharfman lost his job but soon found another with *Sports Illustrated*. After the

Robinson was pictured sliding into home on a 1999 postage stamp.

The Los Angeles Dodgers, and members of all major league teams, wear the number 42 on April 15, every year—Jackie Robinson Day.

move, Scharfman stopped using his Speed Graphic and switched to newer models that used 35 millimeter film. The new cameras could shoot faster (easily capturing sports action), could take multiple pictures quickly, and were smaller than the Speed Graphics. Sports photographers everywhere started using 35mm cameras, just as later photographers would switch from film to digital cameras.

Some of Scharfman's famous shots came during 1961, when *Sports Illustrated* sent him to follow Roger Maris of the New York Yankees. Maris was pursuing the single-season home run record of 60, hit by Babe Ruth

in 1927. Scharfman photographed Maris both on and off
the field. The most historic image was taken October 1
when Scharfman captured the slugger the moment after
he hit his record-breaking 61st home run. The picture
shows Maris, Boston Red Sox catcher Russ Nixon, and
umpire Bill Kinnamon all following the flight of the ball,
which is unseen in the photo.

Taking great sports photographs is often about being
in the right place at the right time. On one memorable
day in his career, Herb Scharfman was in the wrong
place—and ended up appearing in world famous sports
pictures. He, fellow *Sports Illustrated* staffer Neil Leifer,
and John Rooney of the Associated Press were among the
photographers shooting a 1965 boxing match between

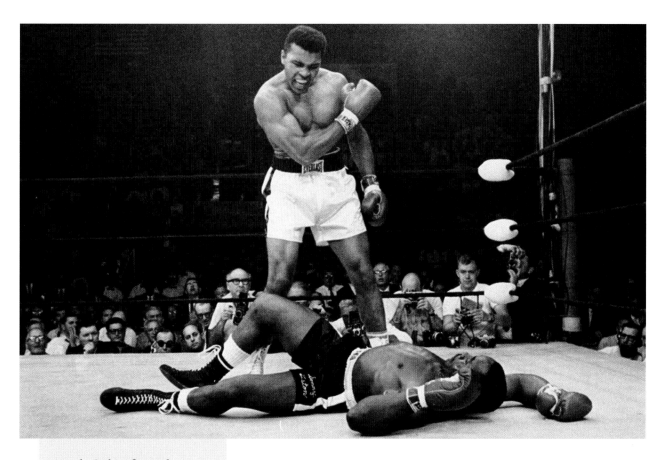

Herb Scharfman's head can be seen to the left of Muhammad Ali's legs in John Rooney's prize-winning photo. Scharfman was in the wrong place for the 1965 Ali-Sonny Liston boxing match.

Muhammad Ali and Sonny Liston. Heavyweight champion Ali knocked Liston out in the first round with what became known as the "phantom punch."

The photographers were facing each other on opposite sides of the ring. After the knockout, Ali stood over Liston, daring him to stand. Liston didn't, and the fight was over. Leifer's and Rooney's photos of Ali standing over the fallen Liston became world famous. Scharfman, meanwhile, could only see Ali's back. Leifer's color shot shows Scharfman's head between Ali's legs. Rooney's black and white shows him to the side. Scharfman isn't shooting the action—he knows he is not in position for a good photo. "It didn't matter how good Herbie was that day," Leifer said of Scharfman. "He was in the wrong seat."

Scharfman's knack for capturing exciting moments in sports, and doing it for more than 40 years, made him one of the greatest sports photographers. Even as younger photographers with modern equipment entered the field, they could not match Scharfman's talents. One example came from Jon SooHoo, the official photographer for the Dodgers. During the 1990s, he and Scharfman sometimes both took pictures of spring training games. SooHoo typically carried two camera bodies and several lenses to catch the action. Scharfman used one body and one lens, staying focused on the action at home plate. SooHoo wrote that "time and time again he would outshoot me … and come up with some beautiful plays at the plate."

Herb Scharfman died in 1998. By then, Jackie Robinson's place in history had long been secure. And in the years to come, sports fans would still talk about his steal of home in the 1955 World Series. *Sports Illustrated* in 2010 ran an article about what it called the top 10 steals of all time. At the top of the list was Robinson's 1955 World Series steal. And while today people can watch the video of the steal, it's Scharfman's photo that turns up again and again. That one instant of Robinson's life became part of baseball history.

To Ellis Cashmore, a university professor who studies sports and culture, photography has played a key role in sports history. Photography stopped the action and let people see for the first time exactly what the human body looked like in motion, such as while running or playing

Robinson's steal of home in the 1955 World Series is the top steal of all time, according to *Sports Illustrated*.

tennis. Before the days of television, photographs—and especially their appearance in newspapers—helped make sports stars national heroes.

Sports history also plays a large part of U.S. history. Historian Mark Naison wrote that professional and college sports have helped build a sense of community across the country. And for civil rights, the battle over segregation in sports, and particularly in baseball, shaped larger U.S. history. Sports, Naison wrote, gave blacks "a platform from which to challenge their subordination." Before Jackie Robinson, a few black athletes had become national

heroes, such as Joe Louis. But baseball was America's national pastime, the most popular sport in the country. Integration in that game carried huge importance for blacks, as shown by the honors Jackie Robinson received.

If someone besides Jackie Robinson had made that steal of home in 1955, would the picture still be as famous today? Maybe, because the play is so exciting, and so rare in the World Series. But Robinson had made stealing home part of his image—the gutsy player who would do anything to win. He had already shown his courage in breaking the color barrier and changing sports, and the country, forever.

Jackie Robinson, often called the bravest man in baseball, stepped up to the plate.

Timeline

1919

Jackie Robinson is born January 31

1920

The Robinsons move to Pasadena, California

1945

Robinson plays baseball for the Kansas City Monarchs of the Negro Leagues, then signs a contract with the Brooklyn Dodgers to play for its minor league team in Montreal

1946

Robinson leads Montreal to the International League championship

1939

Robinson enters UCLA and excels in four sports

1944

In the Army, Robinson faces a court-martial but is found not guilty

1947

On April 15 Robinson becomes the first African-American in the modern-era major leagues

1955

On September 28 Robinson steals home in Game 1 of the World Series against the New York Yankees, and Herb Scharfman photographs the play; on October 4 the Dodgers win the World Series for the first time

Timeline

1956

Robinson retires at the end of the season; he receives the NAACP's Spingarn Medal for his outstanding achievements

1961

Scharfman takes another famous photo, this time of Roger Maris breaking Babe Ruth's home run record

1984

President Ronald Reagan awards the Medal of Freedom to Robinson

1997

Major League Baseball retires Robinson's number, 42; starting in 2004 all players, coaches, and managers wear uniforms with the number 42 on Jackie Robinson Day

1972

Robinson dies of a heart attack October 24 at age 53

1982

Robinson becomes the first baseball player to appear on a U.S. postage stamp; his image also appears on stamps in 1999 and 2000

1998

Scharfman dies February 21 at age 85

2010

Sports Illustrated ranks Robinson's 1955 steal of home as the most historic steal in baseball history

Glossary

caption—a block of words near a picture that describes the image

civil rights—legal rights guaranteed to every citizen of a country relating to such things as voting and receiving equal treatment

court-martial—trial for members of the military accused of breaking rules or committing a crime

discrimination—unfair treatment of a person or group, often because of race, religion, gender, sexual preference, or age

dishonorable discharge—the removal of someone from the military who has committed a serious offense

farm team—minor league team that develops players for a major league team

integrate—to open to people of all races

negatives—photographic images; areas that are light in the original subject are dark in a negative and those that are dark are light; prints can be made from negatives

pennant—triangular flag that symbolizes a league championship

postseason—games played after a sport's regular season

prejudice—hatred or unfair treatment of people who belong to a certain social group, such as a race or religion

segregation—the practice of keeping groups of people apart, especially based on race

subordination—the act of placing someone in a lower position than others

Additional Resources

Further Reading

Doeden, Matt. *The World Series: Baseball's Biggest Stage*.
Minneapolis: Millbrook Press, 2014.

Mortensen, Lori. *Voices of the Civil Rights Movement*.
North Mankato, Minn.: Capstone Press, 2015.

Peters, Gregory N. *The Negro Leagues*.
North Mankato, Minn.: Capstone Press, 2014.

Robinson, Sharon. *Jackie Robinson: American Hero*.
New York: Scholastic, 2013.

Internet Sites

Use FactHound to find Internet sites related
to this book. All of the sites on FactHound
have been researched by our staff.

Here's all you do:
Visit *www.facthound.com*
Type in this code: 9780756552916

Critical Thinking Using the Common Core

The photos on pages 25 and 43 show images of Jackie Robinson with a white teammate. What is different about the two situations shown? What is similar? (Integration of Knowledge and Ideas)

What was the "color line" in baseball and how did it affect Robinson and other African-American players? How did it affect society at large? (Key Ideas and Details)

Who was most likely to support Robinson when he joined the Brooklyn Dodgers? Who most wanted him to fail? (Integration of Knowledge and Ideas)

Source Notes

Page 9, line 7: Jackie Robinson: The Official Website. http://www.jackierobinson.com/about/quotes.html

Page 9, line 17: Arnold Rampersad. *Jackie Robinson: A Biography*. New York: Knopf, 1997, p. 284.

Page 9, line 26: Ibid.

Page 12, line 16: Jackie Robinson. *I Never Had It Made: An Autobiography*. New York: G.P. Putnam's Sons, 1972, p. 132.

Page 14, line 25: Ibid., p. 17.

Page 17, line 11: Ibid., p. 21.

Page 21, col. 2, line 4: *Jackie Robinson: A Biography*, p. 90.

Page 24, line 7: *I Never Had It Made: An Autobiography*, p. 43.

Page 25, caption: Richard Goldstein. "George Shuba, 89, Dies; Handshake Heralded Racial Tolerance in Baseball." *The New York Times*. 30 Sept. 2014. 2 Sept. 2015. http://www.nytimes.com/2014/10/01/sports/baseball/george-shuba-whose-handshake-heralded-racial-tolerance-in-baseball-dies-at-89.html?_r=0

Page 27, line 2: Jonathan Eig. *Opening Day: The Story of Jackie Robinson's First Season*. New York: Simon & Schuster, 2007, p. 49.

Page 28, line 1: *I Never Had It Made: An Autobiography*, p. 81.

Page 30, line 9: Ibid., p. 132.

Page 31, caption: Bruce Weber. "Yogi Berra, Hall of Fame Catcher for the Yankees, Dies at 90." *The New York Times*. 23 Sept. 2015. 23 Sept. 2015. http://www.nytimes.com/2015/09/24/sports/baseball/yogi-berra-dies-at-90-yankees-baseball-catcher.html?em_pos=large&emc=edit_nn_20150923&nl=nytnow&nlid=56738233&_r=0

Page 31, line 5: Arthur Daley. "Sports of the Times: From Force of Habit." *The New York Times*. 29 Sept. 1955, p. 1. 24 June 2015. http://timesmachine.nytimes.com/timesmachine/1955/09/29/83375494.html?pageNumber=41

Page 33, line 9: Shane Tourtellotte. "And that ain't all, he stole home!" The Hardball Times. 24 June 2015. http://www.hardballtimes.com/and-that-aint-all-he-stole-home/

Page 33, line 16: Roscoe McGowen. "Brooks Disappointed, Not Discouraged by Defeat and Showing of Newcombe." *The New York Times*. 29 Sept. 1955, p. 40. 24 June 2015. http://query.nytimes.com/mem/archive-free/pdf?res=9C0CE3DA113AE53BBC4151DFBF66838E649EDE

Page 34, line 10: "Yogi Berra, Hall of Fame Catcher for the Yankees, Dies at 90."

Page 35, line 3: Allen Berra. *Yogi Berra: Eternal Yankee*. New York: W. W. Norton & Company, 2009, p. 203.

Page 36, line 4: Bill Ballou. "Baseball: Upton's Bill Summers was one of baseball's best umpires." *Worcester* (Mass.) *Telegram & Gazette*. 15 Sept. 2013. 24 June 2015. http://www.telegram.com/article/20130915/COLUMN35/309159930/1009

Page 39, line 11: "Dodgertown Dates: March 30, 1953." Historic Dodgertown. 24 June 2015. http://historicdodgertown.com/history/dodgertown-dates/1953

Page 40, line 6: *I Never Had It Made: An Autobiography*, p. 132.

Page 40, line 17: *Jackie Robinson: A Biography*, p. 285.

Page 40, line 28: *I Never Had It Made: An Autobiography*, p. 129.

Page 41, line 1: Ibid., p. 131.

Page 41, line 4: Barry M. Bloom. "Alston's Decisions Tough in '55." MLB.com. 29 Aug. 2005. 24 June 2015. http://mlb.mlb.com/news/print.jsp?ymd=20050829&content_id=1188293&c_id=mlb&fext=.jsp

Page 41, line 7: *I Never Had It Made: An Autobiography*, p. 132.

Page 42, line 14: Roger Kahn. "The Day Jackie Robinson Was Embraced." *The New York Times*. 21 April 2007. 24 June 2015. http://query.nytimes.com/gst/fullpage.html?res=9405E1DA163EF932A15757C0A9619C8B63

Page 42, line 16: Ibid.

Page 44, line 9: *I Never Had It Made: An Autobiography*, p.134.

Page 46, col. 1, line 5: *Jackie Robinson: A Biography*, p. 191.

Page 46, col. 2, line 6: Citation for Jackie Robinson. 41st Spingarn Medalist, December 8, 1956. Library of Congress. http://www.loc.gov/collections/jackie-robinson-baseball/articles-and-essays/baseball-the-color-line-and-jackie-robinson/citation-for-jackie-robinson/

Page 47, line 4: *I Never Had It Made: An Autobiography*, p. 185.

Page 47, line 17: Dave Anderson. "Jackie Robinson, First Black in Major Leagues, Dies." *The New York Times*. 25 Oct. 1972. 24 June 2015. http://www.nytimes.com/learning/general/onthisday/bday/0131.html

Page 47, line 23: Ibid.

Page 51, line 13: Dave Mondy. "How Things Break: Ali fought Liston 50 years ago. Two legends were born, but another was broken." *Slate*. 22 May 2015. 24 June 2015. http://www.slate.com/articles/sports/sports_nut/2015/05/ali_liston_50th_anniversary_the_true_story_behind_neil_leifer_s_perfect.html

Page 52, line 12: John SooHoo. "Something Historical—Herb Scharfman—Spring Training 1990ish." LA Photog Blog. 20 Feb. 2012. 24 June 2015. http://dodgersphotog.mlblogs.com/2012/02/20/22012-something-historical-herb-scharfman-spring-training-1990ish/

Page 53, line 9: Mark Naison. "Why Sports History is American History." With a Brooklyn Accent. 5 March 2010. 24 June 2015. http://withabrooklynaccent.blogspot.com/2010/03/why-sports-history-is-american-history.html

Select Bibliography

Anderson, Dave. "Jackie Robinson, First Black in Major Leagues, Dies." *The New York Times*. 25 Oct. 1972. 24 June 2015. http://www.nytimes.com/learning/general/onthisday/bday/0131.html

Armour, Mark, and Daniel R. Levitt. "Baseball Demographics, 1947–2012." Society for American Baseball Research. http://sabr.org/bioproj/topic/baseball-demographics-1947-2012

Ballou, Bill. "Baseball: Upton's Bill Summers was one of baseball's best umpires." *Worcester* (Mass.) *Telegram & Gazette*. 15 Sept. 2013. 24 June 2015. http://www.telegram.com/article/20130915/COLUMN35/309159930/1009

"Baseball, the Color Line, and Jackie Robinson." Library of Congress. http://www.loc.gov/collections/jackie-robinson-baseball/articles-and-essays/baseball-the-color-line-and-jackie-robinson/

Berra, Allen. *Yogi Berra: Eternal Yankee*. New York: W. W. Norton & Company, 2009.

Bloom, Barry. "Alston's Decisions Tough in '55." MLB.com. 29 Aug. 2005. 24 June 2015. http://mlb.mlb.com/news/print.jsp?ymd=20050829&content_id=1188293&c_id=mlb&fext=.jsp

Cashmore, Ellis. *Making Sense of Sports*. New York: Routledge, 2010.

Cosgrove, Ben. "LIFE With Jackie Robinson: Rare and Classic Photos of an American Icon." Time.com. 12 April 2012. 29 July 2015. http://life.time.com/culture/jackie-robinson-rare-and-classic-photos/#ixzz3VzQwiKnW

Cronin, Brian. "Did Reese Really Embrace Robinson in '47?" ESPN.com. 15 April 2013. 24 June 2015. http://espn.go.com/blog/playbook/fandom/post/_/id/20917/did-reese-really-embrace-robinson-in-47

Derringer, John. "Yanks Win First; Collins' 2 Homers Beat Dodgers, 6-5." *The New York Times*. 29 Sept. 1955, p. 1.

"Dodgertown Dates: 1953." Historic Dodgertown. http://historicdodgertown.com/history/dodgertown-dates/1953

Durniak, John. "Camera: The Old Speed Graphic is Alive and Clicking." *The New York Times*. 15 June 1986. 24 June 2015. http://www.nytimes.com/1986/06/15/arts/camera-the-old-speed-graphic-is-alive-and-clicking.html

Eig, Jonathan. *Opening Day: The Story of Jackie Robinson's First Season*. New York: Simon & Schuster, 2007.

Goldman, Steve. "Negro Leagues Legacy." MLB.com. http://mlb.mlb.com/mlb/history/mlb_negro_leagues_story.jsp?story=kaleidoscopic

"Herb Scharfman, 86, Sports Photographer." *The New York Times*. 25 Feb. 1998. 24 June 2015. http://www.nytimes.com/1998/02/25/sports/herb-scharfman-86-sports-photographer.html

Hogan, Lawrence D. *Shades of Glory: The Negro Leagues and the Story of African-American Baseball*. Washington, D.C.: National Geographic Society, 2006.

Jackie Robinson Steals Home. YouTube. https://www.youtube.com/watch?v=6XY-XshGhMU

Jackie Robinson: The Official Website. http://www.jackierobinson.com

Kahn, Roger. "The Day Jackie Robinson Was Embraced." *The New York Times*. 21 April 2007. 24 June 2015. http://query.nytimes.com/gst/fullpage.html?res=9405E1DA163EF932A15757C0A9619C8B63

Kaplan, Dave. "Yogi Got and Gave Plenty of Respect." The National Pastime Museum. http://www.thenationalpastimemuseum.com/article/yogi-got-and-gave-plenty-respect

Kepner, Tyler. "M.L.B. Report Highlights Sobering Number of Black Players." *The New York Times*. 9 April 2014. 29 July 2015. http://www.nytimes.com/2014/04/10/sports/baseball/mlb-report-highlights-sobering-number-of-black-players.html?_r=1

Lahman, Sean. "Finding Herb Scharfman." Seanlahman.com. 22 Jan. 2007. 29 July 2015. http://www.seanlahman.com/2007/01/finding-herb-scharfman/?wpmp_switcher=mobile

Millett, Larry. *Strange Days, Dangerous Nights: Photos from the Speed Graphic Era*. St. Paul: Borealis Books, 2004.

Naison, Mark. "Why Sports History is American History." With a Brooklyn Accent. 5 March 2010. 24 June 2015. http://withabrooklynaccent.blogspot.com/2010/03/why-sports-history-is-american-history.html

Posnanski, Joe. "Where Does Robinson's ALCS theft rank among greatest steals ever?" *Sports Illustrated*. 4 May 2010. 29 July 2015. http://www.si.com/more-sports/2010/05/04/famous-steals

Rampersad, Arnold. *Jackie Robinson: A Biography*. New York: Knopf, 1997.

Robinson, Jackie. *I Never Had It Made: An Autobiography*. New York: G.P. Putnam's Sons, 1972.

Rosenheck, Dan. "Keeping Score: Robinson Knew Just When to Be Bold on the Base Path." *The New York Times*. 17 April 2009. 29 July 2015. http://www.nytimes.com/2009/04/19/sports/baseball/19score.html?_r=0

SooHoo, John. "Something Historical—Herb Scharfman—Spring Training 1990ish." LA Photog Blog. 20 Feb. 2012. 24 June 2015. http://dodgersphotog.mlblogs.com/2012/02/20/22012-something-historical-herb-scharfman-spring-training-1990ish/

Swaine, Rick. "Jackie Robinson." Society for American Baseball Research. http://sabr.org/bioproj/person/bb9e2490

Tourtellotte, Shane. "And that ain't all, he stole home!" The Hardball Times. 24 June 2015. http://www.hardballtimes.com/and-that-aint-all-he-stole-home/

Index

About the Author

Michael Burgan has written many books for children and young adults during his 20 years as a freelance writer. Most of his books have focused on history. Burgan has won several awards for his writing. He lives in Santa Fe, New Mexico.